The *JET* Alphabet Book

by
Jerry Pall

**Illustrated by
Rob Bolster**

*To all the test pilots who risked their lives
improving aviation so that children's book authors like me
can now fly safely all over the country visiting schools.*

—*Jerry Pallotta*

To Mum and Pup. Thanks for giving me my wings.

—*Rob Bolster*

Text copyright © 1999 by Jerry Pallotta
Illustrations copyright © 1999 by Rob Bolster

Published by Charlesbridge
85 Main Street, Watertown, MA 02472
(617) 926-0329
www.charlesbridge.com

Printed in Korea
(hc) 10 9 8 7 6 5 4 3
(sc) 10 9 8 7 6 5 4 3 2

The illustrations in this book were created in
Adobe Photoshop using a Macintosh personal computer.

Library of Congress Cataloging-in-Publication Data
Pallotta, Jerry.
     The jet alphabet book/Jerry Pallotta; illustrated by
Rob Bolster.
          p.   cm.
     Summary: An alphabet book presenting unusual
facts about a variety of jet planes, from the airacomet to
the zephyr.
     ISBN 0-88106-916-7 (reinforced for library use)
     ISBN 0-88106-917-5 (softcover)
     1. Jet planes—Dictionaries, Juvenile. [1. Jet planes.
2. Alphabet.] I. Bolster, Rob, ill. II. Title.
TL709.P35   1999
629.133'349—dc21   98-46034

Books by Jerry Pallotta:
The Icky Bug Alphabet Book
The Icky Bug Alphabet Board Book
The Icky Bug Counting Book
The Bird Alphabet Book
The Ocean Alphabet Book
The Ocean Alphabet Board Book
The Flower Alphabet Book
The Yucky Reptile Alphabet Book
The Frog Alphabet Book
The Furry Animal Alphabet Book
The Dinosaur Alphabet Book
The Underwater Alphabet Book
The Victory Garden Vegetable Alphabet Book
The Extinct Alphabet Book
The Desert Alphabet Book
The Spice Alphabet Book
The Butterfly Alphabet Book
The Freshwater Alphabet Book
The Airplane Alphabet Book
The Boat Alphabet Book
The Skull Alphabet Book
Dory Story
Going Lobstering
Cuenta los insectos (The Icky Bug Counting Book)
The Crayon Counting Book
The Crayon Counting Board Book
Underwater Counting: Even Numbers

The illustration of the Vertijet is based on a photograph
copyrighted by TRH Pictures and is used with permission.

The jet age began in 1939 when the people of Germany built the first operational jet.

A is for Airacomet. This was the first American jet. When it flew in 1942, the Airacomet did not fly as fast as some propeller-driven airplanes. It was a dud, but no one was discouraged. Everyone knew that jets were the future.

Bb

B is for Bell XS-1. Back in 1947 most people thought it was impossible to fly faster than the speed of sound. A young pilot named Chuck Yeager proved there was no "sound barrier" when he flew the Bell XS-1 at 670 miles per hour, or Mach 1.

C is for Concorde. This delta-shaped aircraft is the fastest commercial passenger jet. It flies faster than thirteen hundred miles per hour. The *Santa Maria* took three months to sail from Europe to North America, but the Concorde flies from London to New York City in about three hours.

Cc

Dd

D is for Dream. This Antonov 225 is the largest jet ever made. It was built to carry parts for the Soviet space program. It is nicknamed the Mriya, which means "Dream." It is so large that at least six school buses could fit inside.

E is for E-3. This is an electronic surveillance jet. The large dome over its fuselage is full of sophisticated electronics known as an AWACS, or Airborne Warning And Control System. By reading the E-3's radar and computer screens, the crew on this jet can identify everything in the air for hundreds of miles around.

Ee

F is for Fighting Falcon. This jet is an F-16. It is one of only a few jets that can accelerate when it flies vertically. The fuel tank holds 1000 gallons. Let's do some math. How long could this jet fly if it burned 500 gallons per hour? What if it got in a supersonic dogfight and burned 2000 gallons per hour?

Ff

G is for Goblin. Before the invention of missiles, the United States defended itself with huge bombers such as the B-36. Military people thought that if the bomber was attacked, these Goblins could drop out of the bomb bay and fight off the enemy. It was one of those ideas that looked great on paper but never worked in real life. Pilots thought the Goblin was goofy-looking, and they never took it seriously.

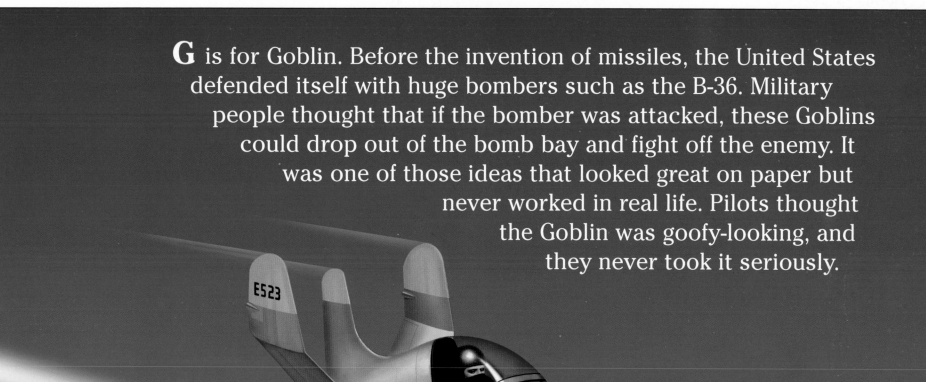

Gg

Hh

H is for Harrier Jet. This British-made fighter can hover in one position, just like a helicopter. The pilot can also change the direction of the exhaust so that the jet can go forward or backward.

Who needs a long runway when you have a Harrier "jump jet" that can take off or land almost anywhere?

I is for Ilyushin IL-62. This is a Russian passenger jet that looks almost exactly like a McDonnell Douglas MD-80, but it has four engines instead of two.

Passenger jets store most of their fuel in the wings. They take off at about 160 miles per hour and cruise at about 500 miles per hour. It takes fifteen hours to assemble an automobile, but it takes nine months to assemble a passenger jet, which is made from about one million different parts.

Jj

J is for Jumbo Jet. The word "jumbo" came from the name of a circus elephant. Ever since then, "jumbo" has meant "extra large." Jumbo Jets are so huge that it is hard to believe they can fly. Some hold over five hundred people.

Did you ever wonder why jets don't crash into each other in midair? Think of the sky as a layer cake. Jets that fly from north to south might fly at 39,000 feet. Jets that fly east to west might fly at 36,000 feet, from west to east at 33,000 feet, and from south to north at 30,000 feet. Each jet has its own layer of airspace.

Kk

K is for KC-10. This is a good page to discuss military abbreviations. "K" is an abbreviation for tanker. "C" stands for cargo jet. The KC-10 holds aviation gas so that it can refuel other jets in the air.

Military Aviation Abbreviations

A	=	Attack	K =	Tanker
B	=	Bomber	P =	Pursuit
C	=	Cargo	R =	Reconnaissance
E	=	Electronic	T =	Trainer
F	=	Fighter	U =	Utility
H	=	Helicopter	X =	Experimental

Ll

L is for Lear Jet. William Lear told everyone he was going to build a jet that people could buy for their own private use. Everyone laughed and thought he was nuts, but Lear proved them wrong. Thousands of people now fly their own jets, and the words "Lear Jet" have become part of our vocabulary.

Mm

Read A Zillion Books

Be SMART!

M is for Microjet. Imagine a little jet, not much larger than your bathtub. Microjets are used primarily for advertising and entertainment. If you owned one, what would you advertise on it?

Nn

N is for Nighthawk. The F-117 Nighthawk
is a stealth fighter that was built to be
undetectable. Its famous triangular shape
is geometrically designed to confuse radar
into thinking the Nighthawk is not there.

O is for—Sorry, this is **TOP SECRET**.

OK, we'll tell you. **O** is for Oxcart. This was the code name the Central Intelligence Agency gave to the development of the SR-71 Blackbird. It was built in a secret facility called the "Skunk Works." This superfast spy plane takes hundreds of pictures per second while flying at Mach 3, three times the speed of sound. The SR-71 flies so high and so fast that the pilot wears a space suit.

TOP SECRET

Oo

P is for Phantom. This Vietnam-era jet is one of the most successful fighters ever designed. More than five thousand F-4 Phantoms were built. Unlike the single-pilot World War II fighters, which were small and light, the Phantom is huge, heavy, and carries two pilots. In a dogfight four eyes are much better than two eyes.

Pp

Qq

Q is for Quick Change. The Boeing 737 is the most popular passenger jet in the world. It has outsold every other commercial jet that has ever been built. When customers asked for a passenger jet that could be changed into a cargo jet, Boeing designed the QC-737. One day the Quick Change can carry people, and the next day it can transport chickens, bananas, books, or even candy!

R is for Raptor. The F-22 Raptor can fly higher, cruise faster, and maneuver better than other fighter jets. Some people think that this is the ultimate fighter. If jets become faster and more complicated than the F-22, pilots could become obsolete. Future fighter jets might be remote-controlled.

Rr

Ss

S is for Spirit. Spirit is the name given to the B-2 Stealth Bomber. It is shaped like a flying wing. If you ever see one fly over you, you might think it looks like something out of a comic book or a cartoon. Let's hope this spooky-looking bomber will never be needed.

T is for Tomcat. The F-14 Tomcat is a fighter jet that has swing wings. The onboard computer extends or retracts the wings depending on the speed of the jet.

The Tomcat was designed for work on aircraft carriers. It takes a lot of practice and cool nerves for a pilot to land a multimillion-dollar jet on the short runway of a seagoing aircraft carrier.

Uu

U is for U-2. This is a slow spy plane. Instead of flying at supersonic speeds, the U-2 is designed for extremely high altitudes—seventeen miles high. At 90,000 feet it is hard to shoot down and very difficult to see.

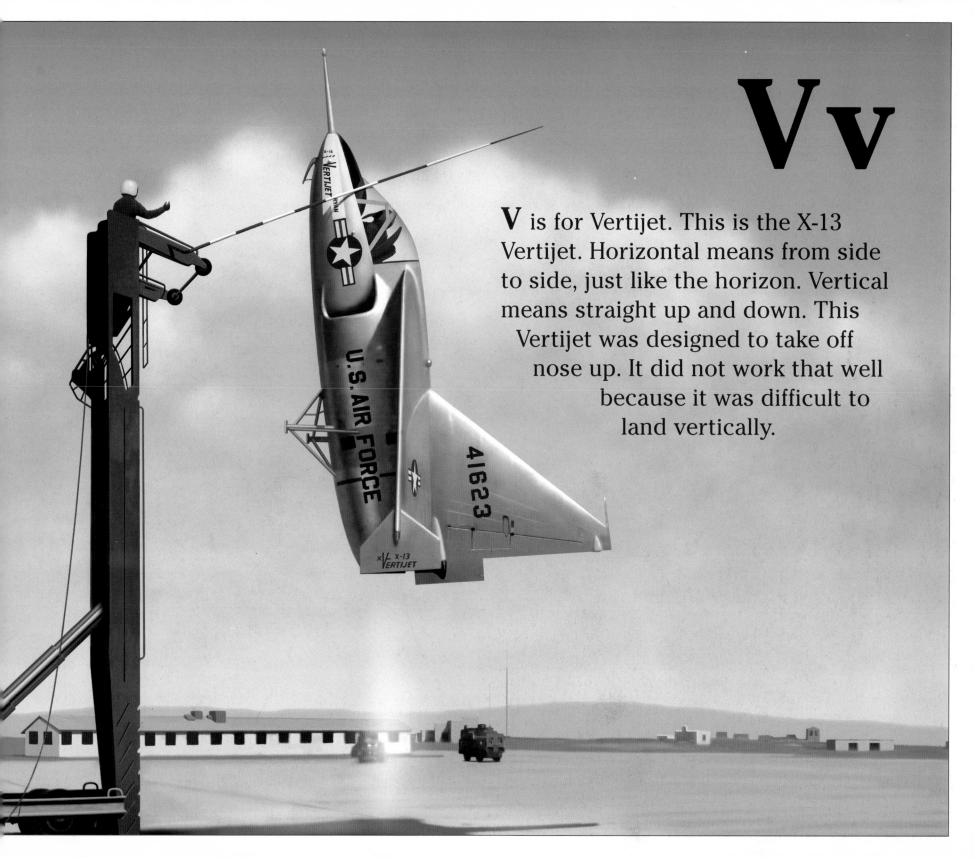

Vv

V is for Vertijet. This is the X-13 Vertijet. Horizontal means from side to side, just like the horizon. Vertical means straight up and down. This Vertijet was designed to take off nose up. It did not work that well because it was difficult to land vertically.

Ww

W is for Warthog. This jet is the A-10 Thunderbolt, but pilots call it a Warthog because it is so ugly. Most jets are built for a specific reason. This "tank killer" has huge engines because it was built to fly low and carry lots of heavy weapons.

X is for Xavante. This Italian-made jet is used to train pilots. There are hundreds of other jet names that begin with the initial "X": the X-3 Stiletto, the XP-87 Blackhawk, the XF-91 Thunderceptor, the XF2Y-1 Sea Dart, the XFJ-1 Fury, and the XF10F-1 Jaguar are just a few.

Xx X is also for X-29A. This experimental jet has forward-swept wings, and it can only be flown with the help of onboard computers. Would you want to be the test pilot who flew this jet on its first flight?

We interrupt this alphabet to show you how a jet engine works. Air is sucked into the front and then compressed and mixed with burning fuel. The hot air expands and blows out the back, propelling the aircraft forward.

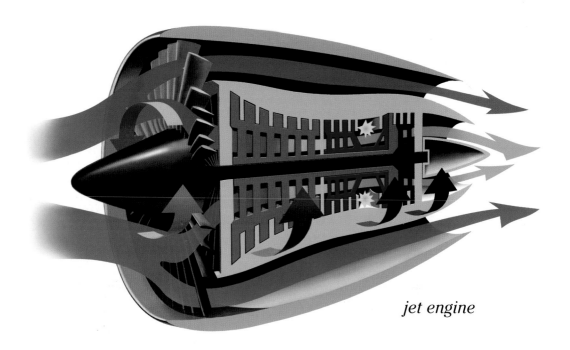

jet engine

A rocket is different. No air is sucked into the front. Solid or liquid rocket fuel burns, and the flaming gases escape from the open end of the rocket. This huge force pushes the rocket in the opposite direction.

Remember the B page? The Bell XS-1 is a rocket.

Yy

Y is for Yak 42. Some Russian jets look exactly like some American jets. The Yak 42 looks like a Boeing 727. This is not a coincidence. Someone stole someone else's design! Just who has been spying on whom?

Z is for Zephyr. This is a French-built trainer jet. Some jets have "T" tails, some have regular tails, but this jet has a "V" tail.

This is what it would look like if a zillion Zephyrs were zooming right at you!

Zz

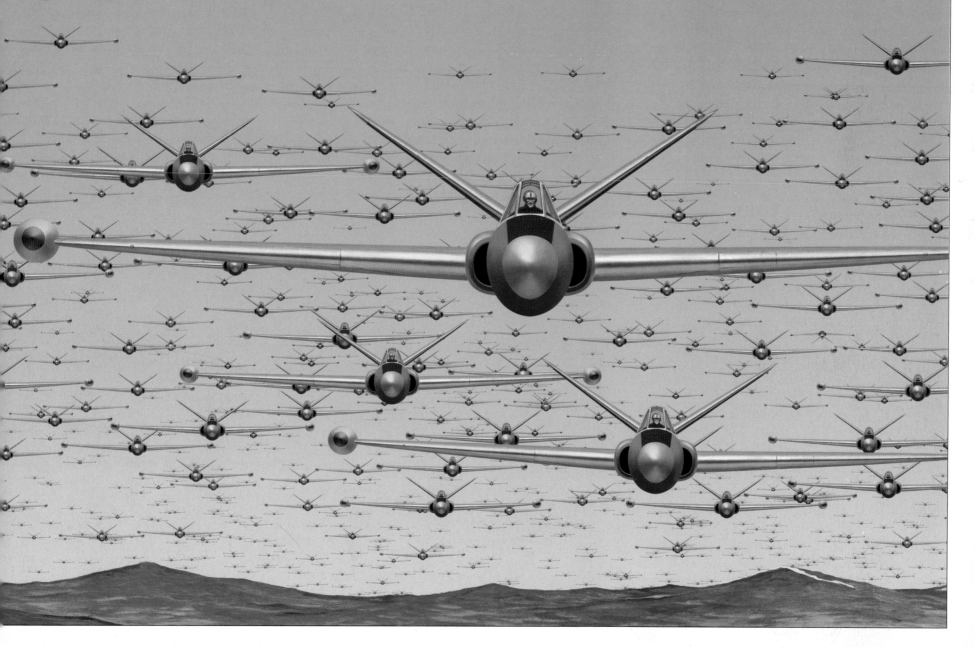

Here is a Boeing 747 releasing a space shuttle.
A new age is here. . . .

ROCKETS!